YOUR STORY IS YOUR
CLOUT
YOUR VOICE IS YOUR
POWER

CREATIVE WRITING MEETS SELF HELP

BY
ROSS VICTORY

© 2021 by J. Ross Victory; Ross Victory, VFTC Universe

All rights reserved.

No part of this publication may be reproduced, distributed, or transmitted in any form or by any means, including photocopying, recording, or other electronic or mechanical methods, without the prior written permission of the publishing author, except in the case of brief quotations embodied in critical reviews and certain other noncommercial uses permitted solely by copyright law.

Created by J. Ross Victory
rossvictory.com

Cover graphic design and color by William Sikora III
sikoraentertainment.com

Chapter images from Canva.com
Edited and proofread by Kate Seger
Special thanks to all the beta readers

ISBN: 978-1-63877-560-7 (paperback)
ISBN: 978-1-63877-561-4 (e-book)

www.rossvictory.com
viewsfromthecockpitbook@gmail.com

YOUR STORY IS YOUR CLOUT
YOUR VOICE IS YOUR POWER

If you were to write a book about your Life, what would the title be? If you burst into song every time someone met you, what song would you sing?

"Your story is your clout! Your voice is your power!" is a book that blends the author's experience as an English teacher, how-to publishing tips, and insights from the author's grief journey to empower readers as writers and editors of their Life, by exploring their inner child's voice as a source of motivation to complete a personal project.

Our inner child never leaves us. Coming to terms with trauma, neglect, and misgivings that have lurked in our lives' shadows is the groundwork for personal development. Pushing through negative emotions by processing the past through written form is a freeing and powerful way to take ownership of our sense of oppression and shift it into an expansive mindset.

We may risk a lifetime waiting for society and our social circles to give our grievances air time. But, if we home in on our scope of control, our voice and expression of that voice through a pen and pad, we empower ourselves and position ourselves to create while others react.

Using quotes from acclaimed psychotherapists, spiritual healers from around the world, and literary geniuses as the foundation of the book—with practical tips the author has learned while publishing four earlier books—readers will discover basic writing methods to enhance their narrative and find themselves overqualified to write *their* first book, legacy statement, song, or whatever they chose *their* way.

If you picked up this book, your past was preparing you for this moment.

And your future self will thank you.

CONTENT NOTICE

This book is not intended to offer medical advice. Creative writing can be a decisive first step in personal development. Still, writing is not a substitute for professional counseling, therapy, hypnosis, or science-based modalities to process and release mental trauma and blockages. Exploration should be done in a safe, non-judgmental environment, including the author's proposition of journal pages and music.

WHAT IS THIS BOOK AND WHY AM I WRITING IT?

The internet, bookstores, and Amazon are jam-packed with articles and opinions on how to write your first memoir. I know. It's a wormhole of sorts; the more you read, the more confused you get about the first step to take. *Literary agent or self-published? An authentic book or a book built to sell?*

The many steps and requirements can feel daunting and unreachable for the average person who just wants to tell their story to experience the freedom that expression brings. This book's purpose is to help readers gain clarity about their first step—the purpose is not to incite confusion.

I am not a psychologist, spiritual guru, or literary genius. I used to wish I was, but I'm not. At most, I'm an artist, a creator, an adventurer, a DIY'er (Do It Yourselfer), someone addicted to finishing for finishing's sake, and someone with the professional skillset to assemble creative teams and hold people accountable for their contribution in a business setting. But I have quoted some psychologists, spiritual teachers, and renowned authors to underscore the premise of this book. ☺

I was a sensitive child whose needs often were not met, a sensitive, empathic, creative child who indirectly learned that my voice was not valuable. Perhaps you were too. Not intentionally or from malintent, but due to a matter of circumstance and perhaps accumulated generational trauma. I sense a lot of people out there obliquely learned the same and believed it. Now, we find ourselves here.

Regardless if our parents were well-meaning and ill-equipped or actual real-life monsters, we find ourselves with a shared problem, somehow trying to get the world to take us seriously while also not being concerned with what the world thinks of us. Some of us don't even know what our voice sounds like or what we stand for or who needs us in the world. This dynamic is an artists' dilemma. My healing journey has led me to write these pages and was ignited by a succession of deaths in my family.

*

Maybe you've been following me for a while, or perhaps you are just getting to know my art. Maybe you found this book from an ad or a family member or a friend handed this book over to you. Perhaps you are curious to know how you can write a book with your own twist. Perhaps you know me or knew me in real life at some point. Maybe you're just curious about what on earth this black man has to say.

My aim is to share a few tips I've learned by writing a book as a personal development tool and to encourage you that if I can write it, you can too. The goal is not to provide a magic pill, nor do I claim a New York Times bestseller is in your future. The goal is to share information and inspire you to find *your* magic pill. Maybe you are the magic pill *yourself* and someone just has to tell you. I'm telling you now!

I'm here to remind you and get that burn in your belly amped all the way up. Your personal legacy depends on it. All of it starts with an authentic, cold, possibly radical expression of your story.

In 2017, I started my writing journey after losing my dad from a mix of cancer, elder abuse, and financial fraud. Little did I knew that this writing adventure would morph into a healing journey that was long overdue. Not only did I learn things about myself and start down a muddy road of unlearning limiting beliefs, but I accessed a level of creative expression that I had not experienced since my late teens before Life began to erode my hope for the future.

I will admit to you that, yes, I worked as an English teacher to non-native English speakers for almost a decade. I've juggled a personal and professional interest in language and communication for years.

While the technicalities of language and etymology have their purpose and are powerful tools to feel (and be seen as) competent, they can be learned and sharpened and are not related to your ability to express soulfully. As long as you know *what* you want to say, *how* is up for debate!

As I've progressed through my creative journey, readers and bystanders have asked me how to access the courage within themselves to tell their stories or even how they could faithfully invest one hundred dollars into their dream they could not see.

Their stories range from overcoming mental or physical abuse, coping with infidelity and grief, desiring to come out as LGBTQ but feeling unable to, coping with addiction, discovering an illness, or wishing to access a higher version of themselves for their personal legacy.

I have learned that the business of "content creation," like publishing books, making music, and creating art, is very transactional, especially when it occurs on free platforms with the goal of pushing it to billions of "impressions." With enough money, you can buy reach; you can buy fame and influence. But remember—all art is content, but not all content is art. Art is authentic and may or may not take the audience into consideration.

We creators spend hundreds of hours, thousands of dollars, and scores of self-induced headaches pouring our souls into our art. Some creators get lucky and get a chance to meet a high-level decision-maker, only to be told how great they are, but they need more social media followers. So, we know that being great, mediocre, or even bad doesn't matter as much as marketability. This is true.

Commercialism isn't necessarily wrong, but our Life isn't a transaction. Mine isn't, and yours isn't either. Commercialism and marketability are not barriers to your ability to create. I'm offering the idea that writing can also be therapeutic. Writing can be the means by which one frees one's mind to become inspired to "play" in commerce because one knows firmly who they are.

I believe the more soul you bring to the marketplace, the better society becomes. Your personal story, your challenges and successes, are worth more than a like or a swipe. And if you're like me, you crave authenticity and applaud people who can just keep it real.

No matter how far you choose to go with your writing, your book idea, or if this book inspires you to take other creative leaps, I'm here to tell you that merely playing back the tape of your Life in a safe, non-judgmental space, like a page or a melody, is a significant step that your future self will thank you for.

I have split this book into two sections. In Part 1, I will discuss the inner child and look at how certain Life experiences get trapped in our mind before you start writing about them and "using" them as motivation to develop your personal economy/marketplace. In Part 2, I will outline practical steps you can take to get ready to write about it.

CONTENTS

PART I - WHO IS THE CHILD INSIDE YOU?	1
CHAPTER 1: The Effect Of Storytelling On The Psyche	5
CHAPTER 2: Surveying Your Inner Child	29
CHAPTER 3: Writing Process And Ngaf *(Not Giving A Fuck)*	45
PART II - READY TO WRITE	51
CHAPTER 4: Ready To Write – Confidence	55
CHAPTER 5: Ready To Write – Motivation/Goals	61
CHAPTER 6: Ready To Write – Building An All-Star Team	69
CHAPTER 7: Are You Ready?	75
Ten Journal Topics To Probe The Inner Child	81
Writer's Affirmations	83
Also Available From The Author	87

PART I

WHO IS THE CHILD INSIDE YOU?

"If you want to keep a secret, you must also hide it from yourself."

— George Orwell, Author

CHAPTER 1

THE EFFECT OF STORYTELLING ON THE PSYCHE

If there is a book that you want to read, but it hasn't been written yet, you must be the one to write it.

— Toni Morrison, author

While telling my own stories, I have discovered that the words of writers and speakers are not only meant to motivate the listener or create an emotional shift but also to soothe the heart of the storyteller.

I found this out some years ago as I grew to become the number one fan of my own writing. I was hugely impressed and entertained when I crafted a brilliant word combination or melody and would burst into laughter and read it back just to turn over the phrasing in my own mind. In essence, you celebrate yourself through your creations. The more provocative, the greater my reaction; it was a test to see how honest I could be or how artfully I could agitate and soothe. Writing can be mental play time.

TYPES OF STORYTELLING

Having grown fond of storytelling in both written and musical form, including how stories can heal broken hearts, it is a no-brainer that storytelling can communicate an idea effectively or create an emotional shift, including sadness, anger, provocation, joy, or any other human emotion. And to do so, writers use different storytelling techniques to reveal the 'heart' of every story. I will explain a few of them here that I used with students in my Creative Writing class as an English teacher.

Rags to Riches

I can't resist the urge to place this one at the top because of how powerful it is among cultures across the whole world. When I was growing up, my dad was an avid traveler and often went abroad on missionary trips. As a curious child, I wanted to go on trips with him and remained interested in travel when I reached adulthood.

As a world traveler, I learned that rags to riches stories resonate with most people, giving us a sense of hope and possibility. Because of this, rags to riches stories are powerful. They tell how a successful individual "made it" against tough opposition. These stories usually depict defying massive obstacles and odds, such as poverty, discrimination, or disability, to name but a few, to achieve fame, fortune, and impact.

A good example would be George Soros. The man escaped the Nazis to become one of the world's most successful investors, a billionaire, and a philanthropist.

Another excellent illustration is Bridget Mason who was born a slave in Mississippi in the early 1800s. When her owner moved to California, she petitioned and won her freedom. After working for a decade as a midwife, she bought a small land plot with the money she had saved in what is known today as downtown L.A., amassing $300,000 in the late 1800s, equivalent to over ten million dollars in 2021.

Voyage/Journey and Return

Some people are simply born under unfortunate circumstances. One moment you are a young person, looking forward to the thrills and adventures that Life can bring, only to find yourself in a deep mess. Not because you failed at anything, but because you were born into a situation you didn't choose or to people you did not select.

How nice would it be to have been able to view our parents' 'profiles' before we were born!? Would you swipe left or swipe right if you saw the full profile of your mother and father before you were given to them? If you're reading this book, there's a chance you may have said, "Oh, hellllll no!"

When the fates align to throw you in the deep end and, somehow, you manage to fight and come back stronger, happier, wiser, and more resilient, it's called a 'Voyage and Return.'

Tragedy

Personally, I am not a huge fan of stories based on tragedy, though they are very effective. Marketing pain is big business. Consider Non-Government Organizations (NGOs) around the world. When they air their "commercials" looking for donations, they put forth the most horrendous images such as starving babies with bloated bellies, sick animals, people with missing limbs, or anything that can drive viewers to shock and tears. The aim here is to tell a tragic story and convince readers and viewers to react positively with a call to action (money, subscription, repost, etc.).

Rebirth

Suppose you have gone through a real-life mess (divorce, sudden death, illness and recovery, estrangement, secret physical or mental abuse, significant financial hardship, addiction and recovery, or the like) and *emerged* from it. Not only did you emerge, but you also became a completely different person with new values and beliefs.

You are unrecognizable in all faucets. In that scenario, you can use the rebirth technique to tell your story.

This form of storytelling resonates with me in a similar way to the 'Voyage and Return' technique. Companies, especially banks, went through a damaging financial crisis in 2008. Even though a few closed down permanently, many found a way back, becoming even more profitable and even more diverse than before the situation, and staying strong. When you see rebirth stories, it tends to feel like the tragic event made them better. The beauty is in the "finding a way back." The beauty is in the *how*.

In the time of Covid-19, which has taken millions of lives and killed off businesses, the groundwork has been laid for even more rebirth stories. If you compare where you were in March 2020 to the person you are now, you could probably write a book about your year in the pandemic! The goal is to pay attention and be mindful of where you are on your own story arc; your Life journey.

If you were going to tell your Life story (year-to-date) privately to yourself right now, which type of storytelling best suits the message in your heart? Where do you feel your story is headed?

Do you feel your story is a tragedy? Are you stuck in rags, waiting for your riches? Perhaps you've been on autopilot and never really contemplated the question. Every moment you breathe, you are writing. Maybe you know you've strayed and have lost your ability to fight to return. Do not be scared to ponder these questions and try not to judge yourself. As long as you're aware that you have a story, you can decide what happens next.

The fact that you're reading this book means that you know you have something you want to say; you know there are others like you that need to hear from you, but you just need some encouragement, motivation, and to identify the proper platform.

HOW STRONG REPRESSED EMOTIONS AFFECT PHYSICAL HEALTH

Strong repressed emotions and unaddressed trauma affect physical health in a significant way. As a young person, we go through emotions we may not understand. As we age, these physical sensations normalize.

In response, you decide to shut down because you want to be seen as tough. This is especially true for men. As men, we are taught to do this and inadvertently bury emotional responses because it's perceived as normal to do so. This programming is so deep, and can be so effective, that ultimately, men do not identify with an emotive response, period.

The repressed emotions become your inner child, which you will have to address and take care of when you are older. Like any child, if this child goes unattended for too long, they will become unruly. They will eventually present challenges and take away the ability for you to be happy, especially as you accumulate more financial responsibilities, relationships, and more complex adult matters.

Maybe you've seen this play out in real life. Someone suddenly makes a huge, unexpected Life change that feels "out of the blue," to the people watching. Or all of a sudden, someone you know has a mental breakdown or explodes into rage and violence. Was this really "out of the blue," or was this inner child being squeezed so hard that they finally blew up?

My first panic attack occurred overseas in Seoul, South Korea. I had moved to Seoul to take a job as an English teacher. One night, I was walking to the subway when my chest felt like it had caved in. I thought I was having a heart attack and quickly lost my breath, falling down a flight of stairs.

I ended up in hospital surrounded by Korean doctors who told me nothing was wrong and that I needed to calm down and breathe. To anyone watching, this was "out of the blue," because I always seemed to "be together." I don't present as anxious or unconfident. But, actually, I had normalized physical warning signs in my body for some time, not knowing they were signals.

Are there any sensations in your body that you have accepted as normal yet you remember the circumstances in which they began?

The question becomes, "how do we address the trauma we faced while young when societal systems prevent us from knowing that trauma has even occurred?" What if we are so socially oppressed that dysfunction is normalized and the concept of healing feels foreign or even silly?

What if we can't see past this month's bill not to mention sitting and taking time for ourselves?

My response is conscious writing.

Conscious writing takes time and discipline, yes, but it's free. Writing is within your scope of control. We tend to focus on external factors like governments, social movements, commercials, opinions of family, but most days, help doesn't come until you face the issue directly. This is not to discount the importance of those entities and voices, but they can't provide the personalized and nuanced care we need.

As we've seen with Covid-19, we can't control the air or predict sickness. However, we can control our thoughts and feelings, and we can adapt habits to make sure we practice honoring our truth.

Depression, sadness, longing, and the need to be seen and heard eventually transcend the heart and soul to wreak havoc on your physical body. Shortness of breath, heart palpitations, sharp body aches, short tempers, the need to medicate with prescriptions, alcohol, unconscious sex, drug use, or the need to engage in abnormally dangerous situations are all signs. Maybe you've been there. Perhaps you are there now.

I cannot tell you how many times I have gone to the doctor for them to say nothing is medically wrong with me. This was a monthly occurrence before I started taking steps to be more in tune with myself.

Have you ever seen someone who looks sick when they have never been diagnosed with anything? Some people say they are twenty-two when they, unfortunately, look fifty-two. Trauma takes a toll, regardless if it's expressed or not. So even on a superficial level, writing can possibly help you look cute!

TYPES OF TRAUMA

Acute trauma resulting from a single, stressful event such as a car accident, natural disaster, breaking a bone, etc.; something that is recoverable from in a short period.

Chronic trauma resulting from repeated stressful events, for example, child abuse or neglect, mental abuse, domestic violence, brutal encounters with police and authoritative systems, back-to-back deaths, racism, poverty and hunger, war, or back-to-back illness. This kind of trauma is the most relevant for this book because it is the one that creates a troublesome inner child and the type I've experienced.

Complex trauma resulting from being exposed to multiple traumatic events. It's like a hybrid, encompassing both acute and chronic traumas. For example, a car accident, a death in the family, and being raped. Complex trauma is very dangerous to the mind and spirit and detrimental to the inner child.

HOW CREATIVE EXPRESSION POSITIVELY AFFECTS THE BRAIN

We can talk about trauma all day, but this book is about how to heal from it. How we experience trauma in our individual Life, how and when we choose to acknowledge it and recover from it, and the method we elect do not need to be justified or publicly debated. Creative expression has positive results regardless.

"What if I'm not creative?" you may ask. "When I was a child, I collected bugs."

Dr. Valerie van Mulukom studies cognitive networks of imagination, memory, and belief systems. Dr. Valerie suggests play, practice, and experience are all things that can foster creativity. Creativity is something that can be developed and cultivated in the proper setting with examples and affirmation. Affirmative environments are key to the motivation to be better.

Watching fantasy films, writing down ideas, brainstorming solutions to problems that affect your daily Life, trying new foods, going outdoors, doing something "spontaneous," and, my favorites, experiencing foreign cultures, eating exotic foods, and witnessing new traditions, are all ways to engage the creative mind. For some, going outside and walking down the street can get the creativity flowing.

Neuroscientist Adam Gazzaley, M.D., Ph.D., says always having something to do diminishes creativity. Sitting still and sheer boredom can help foster creativity. At some point, you get so damn bored that you will invent something to do and pursue. Eventually you will start singing or cooking or something! That was me throughout 2020, and it was the reason I wrote three books and released ten songs. The lockdown made me do it!

Imagine growing up, reaching your late twenties or early thirties and finding yourself depressed or angry for no explicable reason. Have you ever met an elderly person that was just awful with no apparent basis for it? Maybe as you're reading this you are visualizing someone you know who is always angry, and you can't understand why.

Well, society has a way of smothering the needs, wants, desires, and joys we harbored as children. Day by day, year by year, television program by television program, we get caught in news cycles, traffic, the office, and politics.

Then, suddenly, we look around and realize that nothing around us matches who we are. We may look around and feel empty. We are stuck in the consumer matrix being told our stories don't matter if we're not famous. The only entities benefitting from our existence are some corporation or multi-billionaire on a yacht somewhere. Meanwhile, we're on the verge of suicide because of mental confinement.

But how can we realistically give voice to this playful child's needs to stay sane while also generating income and providing for ourselves and perhaps our family? Let's face it, the rich and famous are not necessarily operating in their personal truth. Could you imagine being world-famous for someone you aren't?

No matter what cards we are dealt, our inner child is real and begs to be acknowledged. I believe no matter what social status one occupies, internal peace is possible by observing one's inner child (authenticity) as much as possible.

Before I share some writing techniques that have helped me tap into my creativity, let's look at Jean-Michel Basquiat. Jean-Michel Basquiat used art as an escape from his chaotic personal life. His mentally ill mother was in and out of institutions his whole young adult life. Though very intelligent, he had to drop out of school in the tenth grade and experienced homelessness throughout his life journey.

Starting off as an obscure graffiti artist, Jean used art as therapy and became an admired artist, even famous amongst celebrities, decades later. His creative expression helped him remain emotionally balanced, at least more so than he would have been without the art, until he died at the age of twenty-seven from a heroin overdose.

The point is, whether you are an author, songwriter, watercolor artist, illustrator, chef, or cabinet maker, it's important to release steam by tapping into the energy that only you have.

TYPES OF WRITING AND THEIR POSITIVE EFFECTS ON EMOTIONS

As we discuss writing styles you can use, I want you to keep in mind that the "Why?" behind your writing determines the style and approach that will work for you when telling your story in written form.

I am here to encourage you to write your way out of the emotional trauma you might have experienced as a child. Think of Ross Victory as your cheerleader. Just as a reminder, I am not a therapist or licensed medical provider, but I've talked to many who are and spent thousands working on myself, which has got me back in touch with my writing.

I am advocating for you to become your own creative genius, just like I did, and express your emotions in an authentic, creative way to demonstrate to that inner child that you hear them! You acknowledge everyone who has failed them, and, <u>today, you vow never to let it happen again.</u>

Below are some of the popular writing styles I've used to ease into the book writing process.

Journaling

I remember watching movies, and someone would be writing in a small journal after a long day, "Dear diary..." Whatever they say beyond that remains between them and that little book, most times. That journal contains secrets, pains, and daily struggles that any person, young or old, might face.

With that being said, journaling is a way to express your emotions, fears, and traumas in a book that no one reads but you. It is a way of releasing your own reality without the fear of being judged. I find this type of writing really helpful. In my own journaling, I try not to censor myself. That's the point, right?

Let's be honest, sometimes we have notably obscene and inappropriate thoughts and desires to purge from our systems. We would never want a coworker to stumble on our journal and read about how many positions we imagined their body in or our curiosity about the taste of their "you know whats." I get it. So, make sure you can protect your thoughts, or at least be confident enough not to care if someone reads them.

My dad introduced journaling to me during my teenage years. Sometimes, when I read back what I wrote then, it's hard to believe I'm the same person. There is growth, but sometimes the struggles are still apparent as well. Looking back helps you realize how long it took you to come to terms with certain realities.

You will also notice what you don't write about and *who* you don't write about. Once your emotions are released, though, they hold less power over you. Think of journaling as an emotional bowel movement. A journal a day keeps the psychologist away! Journaling takes consistency and a non-judgmental attitude toward yourself to be effective.

Something I like to do is ask myself if I'm judging what I want to write. Physically, judgment feels like hesitation or the thought, "*Should I write this? What if someone finds it?*" If it's the truth, then a journal is a safe place to put it.

I also try to remind myself to journal when things are *working* and going smoothly.

Memoirs

A memoir is similar to a biography in that it consists of writing a historical account of one's life, and it's all written using your personal knowledge. In my case, my first book, *Views from the Cockpit,*' began as journal entries that later became a creative non-fiction piece; a memoir.

The goal of many memoir writers is to share their life stories with a wider audience. This also helps one become creative with one's past experiences. Celebrities make it a habit to write a "tell all" memoir about lives the public has watched them lived, but memoirs are also for the average person. It's a therapy, just like art, that helps bring out the pain and trauma trapped within you, what we have already called your 'inner child.'

Addressing this inner child using a memoir releases the tension in narrative form. You can also creatively alter situations and create scenarios that give you a more satisfactory outcome.

For example, if someone you loved emotionally tormented you, you can kill them off or leave them trapped on a deserted island naked and afraid, with no food or water. It can be very healing.

Songwriting

This is another one of my favorites! With each song, I can tell a story about a unique experience or express hope for a future outcome. No subject matter is off-limits. While telling a story in a song, it goes beyond speaking to my audience and also speaks to me most reassuringly. This may sound weird, but sometimes I jam or meditate to my own music. You don't necessarily have to write pieces for others' consumption.

Just like a Basquiat expressing his emotions and experiences somewhere on a building wall downtown, music is one of the best tools you can use to soothe your soul. Adele has been known to use music to process traumatic experiences in the past. Thus she released the pressure, found shelter in her own heart, and entertained others while making money. Aside from the entertainment value and a scientifically pleasant-sounding voice, listeners identify with Adele's music and find solace in it—almost like looking in a mirror.

Remember these lyrics, "Hello, it's me, I was wondering if after all these years you'd like to meet?" Most people in the first world have used a telephone and tried to reconnect with someone or reached out unexpectedly. The point is, be true and let your truth reach who it reaches. Maybe it will be the world!

Poetry

We know that poets make great songwriters and rap artists. Why? They have mastered the art of telling a story as it is while capturing or commanding the emotional side of what transpired. The thing I like about poetry is that the writer has the power to direct the emotions of whoever is reading it. Poems do not have to rhyme as there are many "types" of poems, including free verse and sonnets.

If I want to help myself out of a past traumatic jam, I can do that using a poem that touches the right nerves in the right way, exactly as I want it to be. I can use a pen and paper to speak to my inner child and let him know that all is going to be alright. It reminds me of Kendrick Lamar's song, '*Alright*.' He is, indeed, poetic in his songwriting.

Kendrick Lamar is literally speaking to himself in the song '*Alright.*' He mentions how he finally found his safe haven after facing discrimination, resentment that led to deep depression, and other types of traumas. For many, that could just be a song, but it also has a therapeutic impact on the songwriter, it heals past wounds and replaces them with hope.

Spoken Word

Spoken Word is a form of poetry. It's definitely artistic as it requires some creativity to paint a certain picture or bring out a particular groove, for example, including an element of jazz music.

You know, when you go to an Open Mic session and witness many oral poetic performers, you ululate, clap, and enjoy as much as you can. But what you don't see are people pouring out their hearts, emptying their emotional jars to some really safe levels.

The pain, trauma, and abuse we grow up sheltering inside become a heavy burden that needs to be poured out one day. And Spoken Word is one way of doing so. The performer's visual qualities really help ease the body from the pressure, keeping it in good condition while the words take care of the heart. In the end, a previously repressed soul gets freed, thanks to Spoken Word.

Narrative

Narrative writing is mainly based on stories, sometimes fictional, and sometimes not. When you are writing in this genre, you have your central story theme, the main character in it, and several settings you want your story to fit into. Some people create 'fictional' stories that are based on their true Life; they create a personal hero of their own imagination, perhaps someone who will come and save them. This becomes the focal point rather than the pain that they have gone through in the past.

Think about a childhood bully, your feeling of helplessness when you were stuck in a room with them, and the things they said to get under your skin. Remember that? If not, maybe you were the bully.

Being bullied is traumatizing. When you grow up, you need a way of doing away with all that negative energy. As such, writing a fictional story about yourself and creating an imaginary hero—or, if you're dark like me, you simply kill the bully off using some graphic descriptions—creates an emotional safe haven for you.

Remember, the war is staged, fought, and won in the mind. That's why many writers who create these stories find themselves releasing significant pressure from their bodies with each narrative.

Persuasive

Persuasive writing is a non-fiction type of writing where the writer's main focus is to provide logic and make an emotional appeal to the readers. These techniques are used to lead readers in a certain direction or towards an action. Persuasive writing tends to be passionate and anecdotal. Remember passion does not equal scientific facts.

And, when writing to heal yourself, you could do it in a way that encourages you to release childhood trauma through the words and thus free your heart. For example, you present the problem and also the solution along with its impact. Envision an article or story about "How to prevent your child from becoming codependent." You are persuading the reader to adapt your techniques from your experience. By using this technique, you will be completely letting go and untethering yourself from all you went through (perhaps your codependence) because, "you said what you needed to say and how to help it." In reality, that's all you can do! And that, right there, is freedom!

What type of writing resonates most with you?

Now, think back to the types of storytelling we have discussed above and merge two together. For example, you can journal about your rags to riches story. You can write a song about your rebirth from a painful divorce. You can write a memoir about your journey through domestic violence and your return to a safe relationship as a gift for your children.

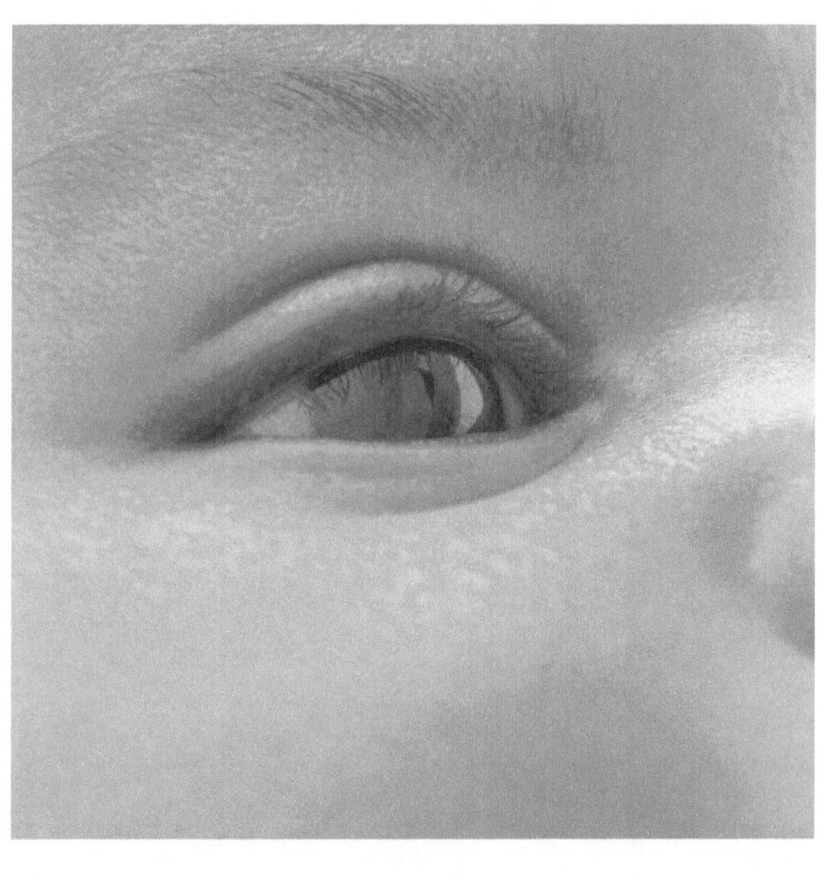

CHAPTER 2
SURVEYING YOUR INNER CHILD

"Not everything that is faced can be changed, but nothing can be changed until it is faced."

— James Baldwin, author

When one chooses not to embrace their inner child, a disparity is created. The disparity is between occurrences in the physical realm and internal needs. These two aspects are either aligned or misaligned.

If you are living with misalignment it's not easy to work things out and achieve consistency. Our body tends to let us know if we are off track, headed in the wrong direction, or operating outside of our truth. Sometimes we choose misalignment so as to not rock the boat. Just keep in mind, this causes internal pressure that must be released before it hijacks your whole system.

My therapy/counseling/self-help journey has taught me that you cannot fully let go of your past pain if you can't hear your inner child's voice or figure out what it desires. Even writing a story will prove difficult if you have not canvassed your inner child. Why? Because we need to know their value systems; their hopes, dreams, and desires to convey an authentic story.

There's a book called *'Personality Isn't Permanent: Break Free from Self Limiting Beliefs and Rewrite Your Story'* by Benjamin Hardy. In essence, the book is about how our identity is shaped by goals. The question I ask you is are your goals from you *before Life put restrictions on you*, or did you set them *after Life shackled you* with restrictions?

I will never forget a short sentence a counselor said to me after hearing me describe my issue. He said, "Ross, you're not the authority of your life." At first, I was like, "Fuck off, bro, what do you mean…I pay my rent, I feed myself, I can plan a trip around the world by myself, I choose who I want to date, I am UTTERLY independent." Clearly, my response nearly 100% ego.

But, as a man, there's a truth about us that many women know very well—sometimes we fall into a trap of thinking authority is solely around our ability to provide.

And we miss the fact that there is emotional authority and spiritual governance as well.

It wasn't until a few days after our session that I could begin to understand that he meant that I had rogue beliefs and mental programs had disconnected me from my truth. He identified this literally within seconds, and I had never noticed in thirty years.

Not only did I not notice, but I was defensive and was triggered when he pointed this discrepancy out. Further, I was paying him a fee to help me point this out. The male ego!

Now, I think of authority and self-governance as a garden. Self-governance is a garden full of seeds that you have planted whose rewards you will reap only after pulling the weeds and turning over the soil of past harvests.

"Life is short. Be silly. Have fun. Love the people who treat you right. Forget the ones who don't. Regret nothing. Believe everything happens for a purpose…and seek that purpose."

−Karen Salmansohn, Author

But how do you fully enjoy your Life when you can't really figure out what your inner child wants or how they feel at any given moment? What if so much separation has occurred that you can't hear them!

According to the World Health Organization, in 2017, 300 million people around the world had depression. Given the current Covid-19 pandemic and the havoc it is wreaking in people's lives, this number has surely increased. I can tell you, with that added pressure, if the inner child is ignored, it can't be good for your health or anyone around you.

Background on the inner child and the voice of the inner child

We've got to first understand the inner child's background and how their voice sounds. Indeed, he, she, or they does have a voice, and it softly speaks inside us throughout our lives—from 17 to 70, from 19 to 90, they're always there as we progress.

Your inner child is a representation of both your negative and positive childhood dynamics. It could be an image of your past Life that hangs on in your heart, an experience that shook your core, or any occurrence that has shaped your adult life.

The inner child is not only the memories of childhood Christmases and vacations to the mountains you took when your parents were still alive or when they still had the money to do so.

It can also contain those darker situations that you encountered, like a creepy relative entering your room in the middle of the night to touch you, or having to be an adult at ten years old to care for your siblings because your parent was an addict, or sometimes guilt and shame around your sexuality.

These shadows live in us, sometimes in the form of retained pain. Some things that affected me were trust issues and hypervigilance. To deal with the pain, we must first know and acknowledge the presence of these shadows.

The inner child speaks through a range of emotions. The inner child is led into action by situations that trigger strong emotions and old wounds from conversations that cause physical discomfort.

> *"I want a man, but I want a man that also wants to embrace his inner child."*
>
> −Paula Patton, actress

This is interesting indeed from Paula Patton. The actress seems to have realized how difficult it is to deal with a life partner who doesn't know how to embrace their inner child, because everybody has one.

You may often hear people say, "Let it go." If we deep dive into exactly what is being asked to "let go," you may be able to trace the trigger back to an occurrence in childhood, or something that happened which you perceived as an injustice, which is also the reason it's so difficult to let it go! You have carried this belief for decades and never processed your emotions surrounding it. What if you can't let it go!? You are trying to sow seeds in soil that is not yours.

So, as a probing question, you can begin to think about what issues, situations, or topics are difficult for you to let go. Beware that the inner child is sensitive and it can be touchy to explore your feelings in this way.

Does the sight of a wealthy person or homeless person trigger you? Does someone's parenting style trigger you? Does a color or a smell trigger you? Do you find a certain type of personality or belief system triggering? Are you triggered by two people of the same sex kissing? Are you triggered by *everything*? The goal is to explore the root cause and come to terms with the source of the trigger.

As soon as you are triggered, you might see yourself reacting angrily to something you did not get when you were young. You might also feel abandoned or rejected. This is very difficult work to explore, and some people may require a professional to help process it. However, with awareness and a pen and paper, you can begin the steps to bring awareness to this child.

I will share a personal example. For many, many years, I was highly triggered when I expressed an issue in my life, and my parents would say, "pray about it." I perceived that statement to be a write-off of everything I was trying to express. I was also deeply triggered by the phrase, "God is good all the time," despite chaos and horror in the world and personally.

"Pray about it," was all they were able to say to just about everything. I read that response as a preference of religious beliefs over what a child was trying to express to his parent, i.e. disinterest.

There was no probing or emotional exploration into the topic at hand. Over time, I stopped sharing and began to resent religion and church environments. I was convinced that religious people and anything associated were, in fact, drones and incapable of interpersonal relationships. So much so that every time I heard someone giving the advice, "pray about it," I would be sent into a terror loop and began cussing them out under my breath.

After some exploration, I discovered that "pray about it" was not an assault or disregard for what I was saying or how I felt. They were participating in the only way they knew how, and I never considered that maybe they were unfamiliar with my struggle, or maybe they believed that prayer was literally the only answer.

So, while I felt unheard, I was not considering who I was expressing myself to. I began to slowly depersonalize and remind myself not to wear others' words or actions as my own. I also had to discover and label the type of communication I needed and seek that out. Awareness inspires accountability. Over time, it became easier for me to hold compassion and understanding and be less judgmental.

Some people even start feeling guilty when something goes wrong. They think it's their fault when they have nothing to do with the issue! Perhaps they grew up in an environment where they were blamed for everything that went wrong in their home by a verbally abusive parent. So, this is how your inner child might be speaking to you through emotions that don't always feel the best.

Why does life give us traumatic situations perpetuated by others and then make us responsible for healing it?

Inner child exercises

This book aims to help you embrace your Life, including your background, and be able to break new ground concerning your personal development through writing; also to help you start writing to your inner child to experience the freedom it brings.

To fully embrace your inner child, you may want to use some of the exercises I have tried and outlined below. Take your time, and make sure you are not reading or listening to this in a chaotic environment. The focus is on you and your story, finding out what your story is and how to reclaim it. You can also highlight or bookmark some activities that you want to explore deeper with a clinical professional.

"Inner child work is the process of contacting, understanding, embracing and healing your inner child. Your inner child represents your first original self that entered into this world; it contains your capacity to experience wonder, joy, innocence, sensitivity and playfulness."

−Mateo Sol, Psychospiritual Teacher

Write a letter to your inner child

I put this one right at the top because it helps you figure out your inner child's core need. Take out two to three photos of yourself during your youth.

- Ask questions like, "Where do I come from? Who are my parents? Do I like them?"
- What are your fears?
- Whom do you live to please?
- What do you spend your days doing and thinking about?
- Who or what makes you feel safe?
- What do you think being an adult is?

Gently explore if your answers are in or out of alignment with the child's expectations in that photo. Alignment will bring you peace; misalignment may hurt. When and where did things begin to change? Did you hear or see something that broke your heart? Was it a person? I'm sorry that whoever was in your Life did not show up in the way you needed them.

When I underwent this activity, I began to notice that I had been emotionally neglected. Yes, my parents were caring people and provided above average lifestyles. Still it appears that I was a sensitive child that needed to be reassured. I also didn't know what I needed or how to ask.

Be sure to let your inner child know they are OK and they have managed very well. Reassure them that they do not need anyone to validate them. Praise them for making it this far.

In your writing, also ask your inner child if you can help them in any way. This will assist with figuring out how to help yourself heal. Make a list of ways you will help. What investments will you make into this child? How will you show up to honor them?

You can write your way to freedom from the effects of your inner child, and no one will ever know unless you share!

Start journaling

We have already discussed what journaling is. Perhaps it is time for you, too, to embark on this journey, document your daily experiences, and focus on the words you put to paper as a way of releasing pressure that's bottled up from years of anger, neglect, abandonment, and trauma. Another way to honor your inner child is to ensure they are given the opportunity to express how they experience the world. So, express it! No one will ever know what you write unless you choose to share. Make sure you remember that! The writing is for you.

Meditation

Meditation is not only for yoga fanatics; it is another authentic tool that you can use to familiarize yourself with who you really are and, in the process, figure out your inner child. I am not an expert and can't give proper advice here, but you can watch YouTube videos, hire a coach, or casually read about how meditation and prayer can help heal your child.

One of the YouTube channels I love is called "Meditation Station." Meditation Station has videos that help you talk down before sleep and get you in a mindset to conquer the day in the morning. You can even branch off into hypnotherapy to help manifest abundance.

Try to Be Open to Lessons from Other People

You will be surprised how many people have been in your situation and how many people can offer valid input into your situation. I know it doesn't feel like it; often, we think our life experiences are unique.

It's impossible to find these like minds until one person decides to be vulnerable first. It's counterintuitive and scary to think that we could live our whole life thinking we're alone when the person next to us has been through similar experiences.

I learned this when releasing my first and second books. It was terrifying and debilitating to share my life experiences with others, including my family, but it's what I felt called to do. Don't ever forget there are almost ten billion people in the world and millions who speak your language. Your tribe is out there!

Thousands, maybe even millions of people can help you deal with your inner child without judging you because they have walked a similar path or experienced similar things. The only way to access this kind of help is to be open to learning from others and sharing where you've been with them. A counselor once told me that yes, it's scary, and the nerves feel like they will kill you, but they don't. Our body is trying to keep us safe while our mind knows that growth is on the other side of that fear. Immerse yourself with examples of people who have gone through it and emerged.

For some people, their inner child is the kind that fears other people and who chooses silence and secrecy, even when in pain. The first step is to identify who your inner child is and what their needs are to become aware of the best ways to help them.

CHAPTER 3

WRITING PROCESS AND NGAF (NOT GIVING A FUCK)

"We have two minds. One thinks, the other knows. The mind that knows goes back many lifetimes. This is the mind of the one heart,"

— Forrest Hayes (2012-02-23).
Na Bolom: House of the Jaguar (Kindle Locations 1865-1866).

Let's say you've decided on your storytelling method. You've decided what you want to share, and you're willing to process your real Life on the page to access personal freedom. You want to take it a step further and turn it into a *manuscript* for a book.

The writing process

Whether it's a memoir, creative, or you are doing persuasive writing, and so forth, the writing process typically consists of brainstorming, outlining, rough draft, editing, rewriting, editing, rewriting, and polishing the final product. I understand it may sound a little tedious; it is, but these steps are the ones I've used with all my books, including this one. You can decide which ones you are OK with.

Remember, we spoke at length about how you must write to your inner self with the aim of healing from your past traumas and negative experiences. I would consider that to be brainstorming and exploring the narrative you want to share.

Tips on how to stop caring what everyone thinks about you

> *"The purpose of a storyteller is not to tell you how to think, but to give you questions to think upon."*

−Brandon Sanderson, Fantasy and Science Fiction Writer

So, the writing process may prove futile if you do it while looking over your shoulder, worrying about what other people will, or won't, say. Remember, their opinion is their business. Their life is their life. There are a lot of messages telling us that others' opinions don't matter, but they never go deeper and say *why* they don't matter.

We don't want to be mean about others' thoughts and ideas, but I like to think of it like this—if the person is not willing to take a bullet for you and prefers to sit on the sideline while you fight, reach, and explore—what value are they to you, *really?*

My challenge has been how to remain graceful while remaining totally unbothered. This requires practice. And you can practice through writing.

Remember, your whole aim in writing this book is to speak the truth to your inner child. *You* are the goal. A better *you*—a richer, fuller, more aware *you*. You are choosing yourself over them. You want to address the child in all honesty about what transpired in the past and give them a voice to help them heal. Therefore, these are matters you ought not to be uncomfortable ringing out. That's the only way this is going to work.

Also, remember that most people do not read as much as they did in the past. So, the likelihood that they will read your piece in full, in the 2021 digital era, is slim. So why not fully express yourself and do the work?

How do you learn to ignore, or at least disregard, what others think or say about you, especially after reading your memoir or journal; especially if they've seen you at your lowest point and will soon have to see you as a survivor and, a step further, a survivor *who's willing to share it publicly*? And what if people in your inner circle played a negative part in the narrative you're sharing?

Let's talk about it!

Stop trying to please everyone—You can't be happy, nor can you fully take care of yourself, while trying to make everyone else happy before you do. I once visited Sequoia National Park and was overtaken by the skyscraper height trees. Trees grow and mind their business; have you ever noticed this? There are hundreds of other trees of various sizes and ages, and the tree focuses on its purpose by growing and bearing fruit with zero preoccupation about what the next tree is doing.

They also do not compete. They are literally centered in *their* being and *their* purpose. To be clear, your healing is your responsibility. Other people's healing, including your mom, grandma, and brother, is their responsibility. I know life is complicated, and we are tied to people emotionally, financially, and more, but how much are you willing to invest in you?

Don't try to be perfect—It's enticing to always feel proud of yourself, but sometimes, I feel like the pressure we apply to ourselves to be perfect is destructive. I am guilty of this one. You will edit forever, but at some point, the editing and reworking will damage the intent of your project.

Know thyself—There it is! We mentioned already how asking questions about your inner child can help you figure them out. The whole aim is to know them better and work better with them because we all work better with someone we know like the back of our hand. We know their boundaries, motivations, hang-ups, and triggers. Love is respect.

Find people who understand you – Honestly, we don't need people who critique our every move. A rotisseur and a baker are both cooks, but the baker probably isn't the best person for the rotisseur to consult on a safe temperature to serve meat. You will have to muster the courage to get out there and look for people that will understand where you've been and, more significantly, where you're going.

In California, we have a restaurant called "El Pollo Loco," which is a Mexican chicken restaurant that sells rice, beans, tortillas, and burritos. How wise is it to go through an El Pollo Loco drive-thru asking for a sweaty burger and fries?

Question your own decisions sometimes—There is no harm in sitting yourself down and asking, "Hey, are you really sure about this? Why did you do this?" A human mind can harbor negative ideas for some time, and without taking time off to reflect on your actions, you may roll down a path fueled more by ego than soul.

PART II

READY TO WRITE

"There is no greater agony than bearing an untold story inside you."

−Maya Angelou, Poet and Author

CHAPTER 4
READY TO WRITE – CONFIDENCE

"Fitting in allows you to blend in with everyone else, but being different allows you to be yourself, to be unique and to be more creative."

— Sonya Parker, Author

In this brief chapter, we will look into the mindset of a writer to see how far you can go in confidently being yourself and allowing yourself to be uniquely creative.

Above all else, when you decide to write anything, be true to yourself. Show confidence in what you want to do; otherwise, yours will be just another story of wasted efforts. There is no need to panic at this stage; you can still develop your mindset into one of utmost positivity. All you've got to do is pay close attention to what I say below.

Imposter syndrome

The Harvard Business Review defines imposter syndrome as a collection of feelings of inadequacy that persist despite evident success. If you suffer from this, you are persistently in self-doubt and, despite a string of successes, you will still feel like you haven't accomplished anything.

That, my friend, is different from being hard on yourself or looking for imperfections; it's just a feeling that someone else is better than you, and you would rather be them than be yourself.

Such a syndrome is usually cultivated when we grow up with parents who label other kids as better than us. People always labeled as inadequate will start believing likewise. In the end, you have fewer chances of being heard in Life because you can't get out there and let yourself be heard, thinking whatever you will say won't be enough. Notice how this is related to the inner child.

Strength vs. weakness assessment

It is not easy for a first-time writer to spot their own writing weaknesses. My first book took two years to complete because I shot from the hip at every step. Now, I know better. Spotting your strengths is also good because it helps you focus on where you are strong and build on that as you also improve on your weaknesses.

I know this is tough, but develop the mindset you spotted in your high school teacher who would always come around and give you that funny look every time you messed up a couple of sentences. It's worth the effort to tell your inner child's story! This can be as simple as recognizing that sometimes your sentences are too long.

Sometimes I use too many adverbs. Something else that I have noticed in past books is that sometimes the story moves too quickly and readers expect more filler language. But my personal, preferred style is to reduce filler sentences and get to the point. You may wrestle determining if a strength is really a weakness or if a weakness is really a strength.

Your story is your superpower (repeat this over and over)

You see? The reason I emphasized getting a grip on your own writing is so you know how to uniquely tell your own story. You can only control the narrative if you really know what you want to say. Everything you say and do is born from illuminating and highlighting the voice of that inner child.

"We all have a story. The difference is: do you use the story to empower yourself? Or do you use your story to keep yourself a victim? The question itself empowers you to change your Life."

−Sunny Dawn Johnston

CHAPTER 5
READY TO WRITE – MOTIVATION/GOALS

"You have to write the book that wants to be written. And if the book will be too difficult for grown-ups, then you write it for children."

— Madeleine L'Engle, Author

What motivates you to write? Is it a passion to change a specific age group's views about a particular subject? Or, are you writing a memoir to heal yourself from past trauma?

Once you develop the mindset to write uniquely with confidence and use your own voice, it's time to create your own writing reasons. If you are not confident, how do you expect to write down goals, or have the motivation to write a book, or even come up with an idea? Remember, these are some of the requirements you need to consider before delving into completing something like a manuscript.

Goal setting and expectations

As a writer, it can be hard to set goals that are straightforward or easy to understand. But, regardless of that, you have expectations with the book you are writing. You could be expecting to start getting some healing, get a certain amount of money in book sales, or change the lives of your target audience. The list is endless.

Your goals for writing and expectations after writing must be in line with each other. You can't afford to set a goal that goes completely in the opposite direction of your expectations. If your expectation is to get healing from trauma, then set goals along the lines of writing a book to yourself in a manner that speaks precisely to you. If you are creating for someone else, you should prepare for unsolicited criticism, critique, and compliments.

Below are some questions you can ask yourself to help conceptualize your idea. You will notice the questions begin with the end goal to help you focus on where you're going.

- Do you want to write about your trauma for yourself AKA trauma dump?
- Do you want to reveal your life story to your heirs?
- Do you want a completed outline?

- Do you want a completed manuscript to shop for an agent?
- Do you want a completed book to look at on your shelf?
- Do you just want a publishing credit?
- Do you want your book to be sold in stores, online, or both?
- Do you want a high-profile review of your work?
- Do you want to be a famous writer?
- Do you see your book becoming a series or film?
- How much time are you realistically willing to spend to accomplish your goals?
- How much money are you willing to allocate to the production of the book?
- Do you want to sell the book or give it away for free?

Tips for time management and discipline

When everything, including the concept, has been laid on the table, the work continues. What follows is a real timeline of the job itself. While setting this, you must be brutally realistic, but also, this is a way of judging how confident you are as a writer.

Have you ever met someone who has been working on a film script for ten years? Sometimes they say, "I've always wanted to fill in the blank." Don't be one of them. No judgment if that's you, of course, but what's up with that?! I know life gets busy and not everyone is a workhorse. I get it…kinda.

I never share what I'm working on until it's 90% complete. The only people that know are me and the creative team (editor, designer, test readers) helping to put it together. Why? If I tell people who I see every day, or jump the gun and post it online, they will expect it to be completed. If I can't complete it, I lose credibility.

Below are some tricks you can use for time management and disciplining yourself to stick to deadlines and goals you set for yourself. Keep in mind that "finishing" is extremely difficult. Very, very difficult.

Writing my book, *Views from the Cockpit,* was one of the hardest personal projects I have ever attempted. Time-wise, money-wise, and personally. The manuscript sat for months under my sofa because it literally felt too difficult. I could not write some chapters without becoming angry or depressed. But, when I released the book, it was also a mental and emotional release that happened to touch the hearts of others and even start conversations.

Please do not underestimate the journey—at the same time, do not underestimate your ability to make it happen. If you've made it this far in your life through trauma, depression, anxiety, whatever life has conjured up and you are still lucid, if you've made it this far in this book, you are not only capable of expressing yourself in written form, but there's a high probability you are "balls to the wall" serious about how, and why, you want to do it.

I have been a 'professional' writer for four years, and sometimes the publishing industry makes books and articles look easy to produce with clever marketing, catchy headlines, and beautiful packaging. But, remember, there is a real person generating those words and ideas, and that person will soon be you, too.

You can do it! The most difficult thing is to stay consistent and inspired.

- First, be realistic about your goals. Don't go overboard and leave space for error and deflated hope (which can be repaired, of course!)

- Manage your expectations carefully and set milestones to measure your success at the completion of every stage. For example, Chapter 1 completed, or 5,000 words written.

- Manage the people around you; some won't cope with you being busy with your own project, they too have expectations from you, and you must manage them.

- Expect and design mechanisms to cope with being burned out. Design mechanisms to help you rest and re-energize. You WILL get tired. You WILL feel like you can't complete your goal. It WILL feel pointless. These feelings are part of the writing process. You can move past it.

- Some family and friends may not support you or might become angry when you start your personal freedom journey. They may say it to you directly or be passive about it. They may feel confused when you decide you want something different. Some may become jealous when you start to become a writer right before their eyes. Some may feel that you think you are better than them for wanting to move past hurt and old narratives.

Something I feared were comments being made either about me personally or the style of my writing behind my back. No one wants to be the star of gossip. But guess what, their opinions don't matter. In real-time, they don't. Why? Because you are so empowered by your story and your voice, and so equipped with ways to write it that if they hate it or love it, it is beyond you!

At the end of the day, you will have both emotional and physical proof (the book) of how far you went to do something for yourself. And guess what? No one can take that away, unless you let them. Expect this and manage it the best you can. Depending on your commitment, you may have to reassess the access they have to you.

CHAPTER 6

READY TO WRITE – BUILDING AN ALL-STAR TEAM

"Only recently have I realized that being different is not something you want to hide or squelch or suppress."

— Amy Gerstler, Poet

After all is said and done, a wise author builds their best piece around a talented and *committed* team. For many of us, writing is a solo sport, but it doesn't have to be. I stressed the word *committed* there because sometimes we need something more than just talent; we need commitment. We need accountability. We need energy and dedication to the project to lift us up.

Have you ever seen a bad movie? Maybe you've left the theater wondering HOW. THE. HELL. DID. THIS. GET. MADE. Well, commitment.

Commitment outweighs production quality, plot, and commercial viability. What a shame that the best creators, people who are one of a kind and positioned for impact, are so full of self-doubt that they cannot finish their project, while someone with half the talent not only receives recognition but is given financial freedom. Really let that sink in.

The difference between these two is that a committed person will give it their all to ensure that the goals and expectations of the project's visionary are met. They are not afraid of going the extra mile to make sure that results are achieved. In practical terms, it is their job.

You will need an editor, exterior and interior designer (can be the same person), proofreader, and publisher. You can use free online tools like Grammarly to check your grammar, but it's always good to have several eyes review your work depending on the ultimate destination for your piece.

While choosing all these team members, you must make sure that they all suit your goals and expectations. Again, don't go to El Pollo Loco asking for a hamburger!

Tips for choosing an editor

As I already said, an editor plays a very important role in the development of your book. Here are some tips on choosing one:

- First, determine what kind of an edit you require – concept editing, copy editing, beta reading?
- Be flexible as you tell the editor your expectations.
- Communicate your intention to the editor to see if they are familiar with your needs. A professional editor will likely ask to see the piece before agreeing to the job.
    - For example, you don't want to hire a textbook editor to edit your poetry!
- Always share how emotionally attached you are to the project.
- Read bios and ask questions.
- Negotiate the price, but don't undermine their contribution. This will bite you in the butt if you expect someone to be perfect but are not willing to pay the appropriate price. Don't give anyone on your team a reason to resent you while working on your Life's work.

Tips for finding a writer's community

Writing can seem like a lonely job, but it doesn't really have to be that way. If you are a new writer, or even a seasoned one, you can find some friends in the writing community. These can't just be some random people you meet in 'internet streets.' They must be people who get attracted to you because there is a high chance of sharing the same likes, values, and writing styles.

The best place to start is to search for Facebook writer groups. I started a writer's empowerment and accountability Facebook group **here**. They exist in high numbers in different genres. Some groups even have a self-help aspect that focuses on writing for personal development.

While in these groups, befriend people who value personal freedom and have walked similar paths or are pursuing similar goals. More so, you surely won't join fiction writers' groups when you are a technical writer. So, think about every step that you take. Again, don't ask a rotisseur a question that should be directed to a baker.

CHAPTER 7

ARE YOU READY?

"Real transformation requires real honesty. If you want to move forward – get real with yourself."

— Bryant McGill, Activist

Now, I am sure that you are ready to write your mind and put it out there for someone to read and be encouraged by your story.

Do you feel inspired yet?
Do you have a title for your book?
When do you want to complete it?
Is the book just for you or you want to publish it publicly?
What type of child would you give your book to?

The more you practice letter writing, journaling, and free topic writing, the more you will get used to the writing process. The final product will always be different than the beginning. Many published writers did not start by writing novels or books as you know them. They began everything with small steps that accumulated over time.

There is a famous adage that most are aware of; maybe you've heard it. It's "Rome wasn't built in a day," which is credited to playwright John Heywood. Some people online expand that quote to state, "Rome wasn't built in a day, but they were laying bricks every hour."

Everything matters. You matter. Your story matters. Your when, why, and how matter. Get a new notebook, grab a pack of pens, and tell your story like your life depends on it.

REMINDERS

- Remember, you can't improve on what you did not attempt to do, so why not start today? Never forget that someone out there needs your story the way you've written it. There are almost 10,000,000,000 people in the world. It may feel like you're alone, but you're not. We are so fortunate to live in the digital era where information and community are at our fingertips and voice command.

- There is a child in you. There is a child in each of us that never dies. What would your life look like if you were to tap into that childhood joy for one minute? How about an hour? A day? A week? A year? A decade? The rest of your life? Can you imagine?

- Consider using Sunday as a rest day. Always remember to take a break, rest, and focus all your energy on yourself. You need the rest. Pick a single day every weekend and take time to meditate, travel, soak in a spa, get a deep tissue massage, and revitalize your mind. Back when I had a regular job, I was on a weekly massage rotation. Now, not so much! Do what you can afford and do something that makes you feel good.

- You may wake up and regret being vulnerable. You may ask yourself, "did I write too much?" "Did I say too much?" It's very important for you to align your intention. You must be mindful of your choices, and this book has hopefully helped you become more aware. Think of vulnerability as stretching. A good stretch will improve your overall workout. If you overstretch, you will cause harm or injury. The goal is improvement.

- Here are some quick online ways to publish your blogs, articles, essays, poetry, and pieces. Platforms such as Medium, WordPress, CreateSpace, and Blogger, among many, allow new writers to publish their literature for free.

"The wound is the place where the Light enters you."

— Rumi, Poet

TEN JOURNAL TOPICS TO PROBE THE INNER CHILD

1. Describe joy. What brings you joy?
2. Do you have a talent? When you were growing up, who was around when you displayed your talent? Describe how they responded. How did you react to their response?
3. What job did you want to do when you were young?
4. What was your favorite school subject growing up? What did you enjoy?
5. What are you passionate about now? Who do you admire and why?
6. How do you cope with emotional discomfort?
7. How did your parents express emotional discomfort toward each other and toward you when you were young?
8. What scares you? How long has this scared you?
9. When I spend time with or see children now, I feel…
10. If you were to give a warning to yourself at seven years old about growing up, what would you warn?

WRITER'S AFFIRMATIONS

Say these affirmations out loud, preferably in a mirror. Try writing them every day for a month. Better yet, memorize them if you can.

1. My story is my clout! My voice is my power!
2. The child within me is alive and well and has a lot to say. I will honor their voice once and for all.
3. Today, I am so empowered to tell my story that I can barely contain myself.
4. Only those with courage can access success. I have courage. I am courage.
5. My words have the power to change hearts and minds.
6. My mind is bursting with creativity and ideas about how to tell my story.
7. Hidden valleys and mountains of success are all around me. I will meet the universe halfway by harnessing my truth and sharing it with the world.
8. I am thankful that so many people have been touched by my story.
9. I am not fully aware of how great I am.

10. I water my mind with positivity and expansion daily.
11. I am so grateful that I took a chance on myself.
12. Writer's block is a natural part of the writing process.
13. What I write is not up to anyone.
14. I don't know why I didn't believe in my voice for so long, but now I know better, and I will never give up on myself again.
15. Someone else's success is not my demise. They are my motivation and inspiration!
16. New thoughts and ideas are all around me.
17. Writing is like breathing.
18. Life occurs in ebbs and flows. When I'm tired, I will rest. When I'm energized, I will write.
19. When I'm telling my story, I am aligned with who I am.
20. My truth is not up to you.

Ross Victory is a singer/songwriter turned author from Southern California. He is the author of the award-winning non-fiction books *Views from the Cockpit: The Journey of a Son* and *Panorama: The Missing Chapter.* When Ross isn't writing or singing, he enjoys traveling and cars.

Learn more: rossvictory.com

ALSO AVAILABLE FROM THE AUTHOR

www.ingramcontent.com/pod-product-compliance
Lightning Source LLC
LaVergne TN
LVHW091603060526
838200LV00036B/980